Blind Hope

A Motivational Memoir of Going Through to Get To

By: Kimberly Holmes

Blind Hope: A Motivational Memoir

©2018, Kimberly Holmes
This book was created in collaboration with Eryka Parker of Lyrical Innovations, LLC
www.Lyricalinnovationsllc.com

All rights reserved. Printed in the United States of America. No part of this book may be used or reproduced in any manner whatsoever without written permission except in the case of brief quotations embodied in critical articles or reviews.

This book is a work of non-fiction. All content within this work of non-fiction is based on true events. The author is not a doctor. Please do not confuse the diagnoses and personal affirmations of the author with professional medical advice. All content included in this book is the property of Kimberly Holmes and shall not be used without her permission. Most names have been changed and in some cases event details were condensed.

Questions or comments can be directed to info@lyricalinnovationsllc.com

Book cover design by Ian Robinson

Edited by: T. Gigax, Fresh Eyes Reading

Author photo copyright © 2018 by: Jackie Hatfield, taken at King's Gym. All Rights Reserved.
T-shirts designed by Dominique Render

First Edition

Topics

Introduction 1

Round 1: The Trauma That Caused It All 3

Round 2: My Diagnosis 7

Round 3: My Search for Normalcy 12

Round 4: My Fight to be Heard 18

Round 5: My Rebellious Emancipation 23

Round 6: Pulling on My Mommy Gloves 28

Round 7: It All Falls Down 35

Round 8: The Fade to Black 43

Round 9: The Rebirth 48

Round 10: The Main Event...Getting My Kids Back 55

Time to Train 59

Best Practices for Developing and Maintaining a Positive Mindset
.... 60

Best Practices for Success 61

The Recap 62

About the Author 64

Introduction

I have been completely blind for the past 12 years, due to a condition called diabetic retinopathy. Dealing with my blindness has certainly been the hardest challenge I have faced, but I am in *no way* a victim. So, if you're looking for a sob story, you can close this book now and find another. What you will find is the motivational memoir of an inspired mother, sister, daughter, and friend. After reading this, you will find yourself more informed about diabetes and some of the severe medical conditions that can come with it. If diabetes goes untreated – blindness is one of the many life-altering complications that can arise. You will learn more about the importance of self-care and self-advocacy. You will find content that will motivate you to do more for yourself and others and to never take no for an answer – regardless of who provides that answer. You will also learn some best practices for keeping a positive mindset, despite the type of obstacles that are placed in your path. God will always give you the tools you need to face and conquer ***all*** obstacles if you choose to believe in Him and in yourself.

Life is not easy - take it from me. Nevertheless, I have found that my life mantra of, "you have to go through to get to," which was provided by my Dad – who is a bishop – positively impacts my life every day. If you face each obstacle with the attitude that you must get through it to equip yourself with the tools for future experiences, you will always be blessed to later find the lesson in what you are enduring. Turning those lessons into tools of empowerment will get you far, and you will live life with fewer regrets. This is exactly how I, a blind person, came to have clearer vision than most people with sight.

This story has been told strictly from my own perspective. I believe it's important to preserve your memories specifically as you remember experiencing them. With that said, I would like to state that I have amazing parents, family, and friends. They have been supportive of me during my childhood and throughout adulthood and have been a collective backbone for me. As you explore the details of my life story within these pages, please keep in mind that my experiences are my own and do not include backstories or viewpoints of others in my life.

Now, if you are ready to begin, there are a few requirements. Take my hand, close your eyes, and open your mind as I lead you on this insightful journey of Blind Hope.

Welcome. I am more than honored to be your guide.

Deuteronomy 6:4 Hear, O Israel: Yahweh is our God, Yahweh is one.

Shema Israel Yahweh Elohim Yahweh Echad
Most Humbly,
Kimberly Holmes

The Trauma That Caused It All

The first time I inched into the ring as an amateur boxer, at the tender age of 9, it was a result of being tag teamed. I wasn't expecting to engage in a fight so early in my boxing career, but my guardian turned teammate was unable to defend herself. She was desperate and in need of my help. So, I laced up my shoes and pulled on my gloves, unsure of how this fight would go. I didn't understand what I was seeing, but I knew that what was happening should not have been taking place. The bell rang. Shell-shocked, I timidly danced around the ring for a bit, but then I quickly jumped into action ....

I stood frozen with my feet planted heavily on the living room carpet. My thoughts were flickering at a rate of one thousand miles per minute, and no matter how hard I tried, I couldn't will my body to move. My stepfather's hands were firmly planted around my mother's neck as he dragged her, kicking and screaming up the stairs.

"Call nine-one-one, Kim! Now!" The terror in her voice matched the look on her face, which was one of sheer alarm. I looked up at my stepfather's face and saw distant eyes dazed by a drug-induced state.

My two-year-old little sister clung to my legs. I heard my brother playing with his friends just outside the door, completely unaware of the turmoil that ensued within our home. He was a year older and would know what to do. But I knew I didn't have time to go out there and explain. I had to move. I finally moved my leaden feet and shuffled over to the kitchen. Reaching for the cordless phone, I followed my mother's instructions.

"Nine-one-one. What is your emergency?"

Help! Please help me! My mother is being attacked by my sister's father, I thought but the words would not come out. My heart beat wildly in my chest and my mouth felt like it was lined with cotton. I ran my thick tongue over my dry lips, as my chest heaved in and out.

"Nine-one-one. What is your emergency?" the operator repeated.

The phone slipped out of my sweaty palms, forcing me to end the call. I then went to check on my sister. A few seconds later, the phone rang.

I walked over to answer it and heard the same woman's voice on the line. "An emergency call was just placed from this phone number. Is there an emergency?"

I blinked as I gripped the phone tightly. *Yes! Yes, there's an emergency! Get over here right now,* I thought, but, once again, my lips refused to move.

Five minutes later, blue and red flashing lights filled our living room as I held my sister in my lap, singing to drown out the screams above us.

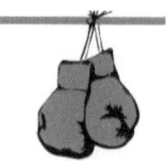

Highlight Reel: This was one of the scariest moments of my childhood. Witnessing my mother in that predicament with no one else there left me feeling helpless, frantic, and alone. I was young, afraid, and very confused about what I was witnessing, but I knew that I had to move past my fear and act quickly in order to save my mother. In hindsight, that experience gave me the chance to understand what my children would have to experience later as my advocates.

Please take some time to reflect on this message, then complete the exercises on the following pages.

Exercise 1:1

Embracing the Lesson: Think about a time when you had to face a challenge that seemed impossible. Whether it was stepping in as an advocate for someone or standing up for yourself against a bully, a difficult boss, or someone that held an intimidating position. Were you able to show up the way you would have liked? Why or why not? What would you have done differently?

_____
_____
_____
_____
_____
_____
_____
_____
_____
_____
_____
_____
_____
_____
_____
_____
_____
_____
_____
_____
_____
_____

Exercise 1:2

Displaying Gratitude: Has there ever been a time when people have stood in the gap for you? If so, put yourself in their shoes and think about the courage it may have taken for them to step in as your advocate. Jot down ideas of what may have been going through their heads at the time. If these people are still in your life, write them a thank you note, send a card, or pick up the phone and thank them for what they did or are still doing in your life.

_____
_____
_____
_____
_____
_____
_____
_____
_____
_____
_____
_____
_____
_____
_____
_____
_____
_____
_____
_____
_____
_____
_____
_____
_____
_____
_____
_____

My Diagnosis

Two Weeks Later

I stepped back into the ring shortly after. I laced up my shoes and pulled on my gloves once again, unsure of who or what I would be fighting this time. I was still processing the graphic details of what I had witnessed so vividly. But I also knew that something was physically wrong with me. I just couldn't pinpoint what it was. What I did know was that I was going to give this next fight my very best shot. I knew I would emerge victorious either way.

"Kim! Why didn't you tell me you had to throw up?!"

I wiped my mouth as tears sprung from my eyes. I didn't mean to make a mess in my mother's car, but it came up too quickly for me to react. I sat back in the seat and closed my eyes for the rest of the silent ride to the house. My stepfather remained in the house with us, but not for much longer, as my mother was in the process of securing somewhere else for us to stay. My biological father was not in my life at the time, as his incessant drug use forced my mother to leave him.

Blind Hope

Once we arrived home, I lay down on the couch with a blanket covering me but, as the days passed, my health did not improve. I continued to feel nauseous and couldn't keep anything down for three days. Dark rings encased my sunken eyes; I experienced dry mouth, and I couldn't sit up without enduring severe stomach pains. My mother took me to the doctor, and he diagnosed me with the stomach flu and sent me back home. A few days later, my symptoms persisted, and I became extremely fatigued and dehydrated.

I eventually fell into what we later discovered was a brief diabetic coma and woke up in Rainbow Babies and Children's Hospital with a blood glucose level of 1300. It was 1987 and, back then, the average person's sugar level was no more than 120, so my values were the highest record at that time. The medical team declared it a miracle that I was still alive with such an accelerated glucose level. The doctors later diagnosed me with Type 1 diabetes, also known as juvenile diabetes. Simply put, my pancreas was not producing enough insulin to break down the sugar in my blood. Consequently, I required insulin injections from that point on to help regulate my blood sugar.

Diabetes was a heavyweight contender that had worked its way up the ranks, conquering countless opponents before me. Here I was a young girl who had only one bout to her name. How in the world would I face this monster alone – and win?

I remained under close observation in the hospital for almost three weeks while the medical staff ran additional tests. At that time, the medical industry had much to learn regarding the wide range of complications associated with diabetes. They focused on foot care, managing my diet and regulating my insulin intake. I could return to school once my blood sugar stabilized.

I was disappointed by the news of my health, but, despite it all, I had won my first bout in the ring at the tender age of nine. I had emerged from my coma, was diagnosed and treated and was on my way to learning more about my disease. Little did I know I would fight dozens of rounds thereafter.

Back at school, I received a very warm welcome from my classmates, teachers, and administrative staff. I cherished the happiness and relief I experienced as a result of my improved health state. However, I was only experiencing a "honeymoon period" and more complications and issues lay undetected.

At the conclusion of my 4th grade school year, my mother enrolled me in a diabetic summer camp where I learned more about self-care through fun and educational activities. Being surrounded by other children with diabetes-related complications similar to what I experienced had a positive effect on my self-esteem. It was beneficial to be able to speak to other children who understood how it felt to live with juvenile diabetes.

The camp counselors focused on educating campers on health management while allowing us to have fun and enjoy our childhood. I participated in fun recreational activities like boating, canoeing, scuba diving, swimming, and archery. The summer camp was the highlight of my childhood, and I attended between the ages of 10 to 15. My experiences at the camp were the very first bricks laid on my path to finding hope, despite the severity of my situation.

My mother eventually started dating again and fell in love. She married a man I still call Dad to this day. I will refer to him as Bishop from now on. Mom and Bishop were often hard on me and, consequently, I often felt like I couldn't open up to them about what I was feeling and what was happening in my life. So, I turned to my best friend, Tori, as my confidant. Tori was easy to confide in about my feelings and the details of my condition because I fully trusted her not to judge me.

Do you have a go-to person in your life? If not, make it a point to find a positive outlet. You can start a journal, admire some art, read self-help books, or start a blog on the subject. When you're going through things that are stressful for you, it's important to find a healthy release.

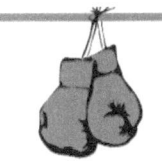

Highlight Reel: I experienced drastic life changes during the early years of my life. When your primary goal is fitting in with your peers and having fun, a serious disease like diabetes can be a heavy burden to carry.

Exercise 2:1

The Power of Retrospect: Reflect on the events that led up to your current undesired circumstances. How did you feel when you were facing life-changing news? If it was a result of poor choices, what lesson did you learn to make better choices in the future? If it was due to factors that were out of your control, how can you create a plan to move forward and make the best of your situation?

_____
_____
_____
_____
_____
_____
_____
_____
_____
_____
_____
_____
_____
_____
_____
_____
_____
_____
_____
_____

Exercise 2:2

It Takes a Village: Once you move through the initial shock of a life-altering change, the next step is to seek help. If you are facing a physical or mental illness or a major circumstance that you know little about, you should seek an advocate who can educate you on the matter. If you are facing a temporary life obstacle like financial hardship, you should seek advice from an expert or a community center that can refer you to free counseling services. List the support you need below and map out your plan to empower yourself with information.

_____
_____
_____
_____
_____
_____
_____
_____
_____
_____
_____
_____
_____
_____
_____
_____
_____
_____
_____
_____
_____
_____
_____
_____
_____
_____

My Search for Normalcy

Despite the wonderful things I learned during my time at summer camp, I struggled with processing the complications that diabetes placed in my life. For instance, I often watched my friends at school and in my neighborhood enjoy candy, juice, chips, and other snacks that most children crave. During my middle school years, I found myself sneaking off to enjoy candy and sugary drinks at school and home. I was fully aware of my doctor's warning to avoid unhealthy food, especially sweets. Nevertheless, I refused to listen. Because of my illness, I developed the attitude that I had suffered enough and wanted to have fun and blend in with my friends. For me, it was about being a kid and being carefree – even if it involved something as trivial as eating junk food.

One day at school, one of my classmates who knew about my illness took notice of my poor eating habits. Out of concern, she informed my teacher about my condition and dietary restrictions. My teacher immediately called my parents and updated them on what I was doing at school. From that point on, my diet and glucose levels were closely monitored to ensure I remained compliant and more importantly, healthy.

Kimberly Holmes

I didn't feel that my eating habits were that big of a deal and certainly didn't think that I was doing anything life-threatening. That said, being closely supervised was frustrating and annoying. I knew that my family and teachers were looking out for me, but I wished that everyone would stop monitoring me and let me live my life. Even things as trivial as a visit to the dentist's office resulted in my being hospitalized. In high school, I attempted to play sports, but my health complications restricted me from participating. My delicate life was often unpredictable, and stressful. I felt like I needed to live in a bubble.

Under the care of Bishop, who was very stern, I often longed desperately to just be a kid. We were always at church and expected to stay in the house. At the age of 12, it was my responsibility to watch my younger brother and sister indoors while my friends played freely outside. Grateful for the days that I felt good enough to go outside, I wanted to join my friends and play with them, leaving my cares behind. Due to my parents' expectations of me to be my siblings' caregiver, I often felt as though I was their mother. I felt stuck and resentful because I couldn't fully experience my childhood due to my illness and responsibilities. Don't get me wrong, I appreciated the times I did manage to spend outside playing. I also enjoyed going to summer camp and had some wonderful experiences there. But it just didn't seem to be enough, and I had regrets regarding how my childhood was spent.

At 14 years old, I wanted my own money, responsibilities, and, most importantly, <u>more time to myself</u>. So, I found a job. I knew that it would be up to me to figure out my future and set the guidelines for my life. If I wanted something, I would have to make it happen instead of just sitting around and waiting for it to be hand-delivered to me. My childhood and my illness gave me the determination to get out of the house and live on my own when the time came.

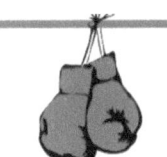

Highlight Reel: Living with a serious illness at a young age drastically changed my mindset. I came to terms with my disease and the lifestyle sacrifices I had to make because of it. I also came to terms with having strict parents and with the fact that, sometimes, life isn't always fair. I also realized that I couldn't just react to what my life handed me. I had to be proactive in order to manifest the positive things that I wanted in my life. I was ready to step into the boxing ring on my own damn terms. Gloves up!

Round 3
Moment Of Reflection

Exercise 3:1

The Need to Fit In: Reflect on a time when you saw the unique features God blessed you with as burdensome. Was that attitude due to poor self-image or the thoughts and opinions that were projected onto you from your environment? In retrospect, was it a legitimate issue or a perceived one? Overall, are you grateful for the experience and how it helped shape your life? Please elaborate below.

_____
_____
_____
_____
_____
_____
_____
_____
_____
_____
_____
_____
_____
_____
_____
_____
_____
_____
_____

Blind Hope

Exercise 3:2

Changing the Game: Reflect on a time when you took the reins to change an undesirable personal situation for the better. How did you conclude that the decision was in your best interest? What was the deciding factor? Do you regret making the decision? Why or why not?

My Fight to be Heard

At the age of 16, my weight had fallen extremely low after a month of experiencing a loss of appetite and an inability to eat. I experienced severe stomach pains and nausea and food was no longer as appealing. I had to hold my pants up around my waist while walking around school because they were falling off me. I often lain on the floor with my books during my classes because I had severe muscle loss and was too weak to sit up in class. My lack of appetite and dramatic weight loss left my parents feeling just as concerned about my mental well-being as they were with my overall health. Therefore, they decided to take me in to be evaluated. The psychologist automatically assumed that I had an eating disorder. He suggested they admit me to the psychiatric ward of the hospital against my will. My parents agreed, and before I knew it, I was admitted.

That was a punch that landed far below the belt. It hurt and disappointed me that my parents ignored my protests as well as my explanation about my situation. It seemed as though they had totally shut me out, disregarded my feelings, and refused to hear me. I was already struggling with low self-esteem and felt alienated from my friends and family due to my diabetes. As I mentioned previously, my illness severely limited my participation in athletics which left me with no sense of accomplishment, despite my passion to push myself in everything that I did.

Despite the restrictive and prohibitive limitations my illness placed on me, I refused to become a victim of my circumstances. I was not in agreement with my mental illness diagnosis and did not see the need to be medicated. The stress from my situation eventually led to more flare ups associated with diabetes.

While in the hospital, I lacked an appetite. I would look at the food and just the sight of it would make me sick. I would call my mother on the pay phone, insisting that I had a severe stomach issue and that I wasn't mentally ill. I knew that my lack of appetite was not a psychological disorder, although everyone at the hospital tried to convince me otherwise. Eventually, they insisted that I use a feeding tube since I was not interested in eating. Reluctantly, I gave my consent. I was given Ensure and was able to keep it down.

Being able to adequately take in nutrients was a win for both the medical staff and me. However, the hospital stood firm in their belief that I suffered from mental illness and prescribed Prozac to take each morning. I would take the pill from them and hold it under the side of my tongue until they let me use the bathroom. While in there, I would flush it. **I was playing possum, just going through the motions, knowing that my opportunity to strike back would come soon–if I played along with their rules.** After a few weeks of being on the feeding tube and their assumption that I was taking my daily medicine, the doctor finally conceded to my unyielding requests to have my stomach examined.

Afterward, the test results showed that my intestines were impacted with feces. No one was monitoring my bowel movements while I was there. If they had done so, they would have known that I was severely constipated. Unfortunately, they already decided that I was mentally ill and didn't deserve to be heard. From that point on, I was given laxatives, which helped me get some relief. The pain in my intestines went away, my appetite slowly returned, and I gradually began to desire food again.

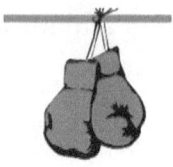 **Highlight Reel:** Despite the circumstances, I never gave up on my decision to reject the labels that others tried to place on me. I chose the narrow path of forcing them to listen instead of the easier path of giving in to something that I didn't believe. **I have never done so much bobbing and weaving in my life! Everything and everyone seemed to be designed against me and I was fully engaged in the fight of my life.** Trying to convince the world that I did not belong in their categories took a lot of determination and self-assuredness at a young age. But I succeeded and I am so grateful that I was able to embrace and utilize the voice that God has given me. **Prognosis blocked!** To God be the glory. **I won another round in the fight of my life.**

Exercise 4:1

Hear Me Roar: Reflect on a time when you felt unable to express yourself. Maybe you felt as if no one was listening to what you had to say. Were you able to get your point across or did you eventually give up? Either way, it had an impact on your life. Would you have done anything differently? Journal about your experience below and how it made you feel.

_____
_____
_____
_____
_____
_____
_____
_____
_____
_____
_____
_____
_____
_____
_____
_____
_____
_____
_____
_____

Exercise 4:2

The Power of External Influences: Reflect on a time when you felt unsure of what your purpose was. Has anyone ever knocked you off course with their doubts or negative behavior? How did it feel to be impacted in that way? What did you learn about yourself in the process?

My Rebellious Emancipation

My mother brought my schoolwork up to the hospital and I worked with the hospital tutors on my assignments whenever I needed assistance. Thankfully, I was able to complete my homework and graduate on time.

Once my appetite returned, I asked my mother to cook and bring food with her whenever she would visit because the sustenance at the hospital was not appetizing in the least. Unfortunately, the medical staff insisted that I eat the food there and prohibited any outside food. I eventually complied and ate just enough food to meet the requirements for my release.

After my discharge, I began to reflect on all that I had been through and what it all meant. For a girl so young, my recent struggle felt far too heavy to bear at times. I was a young child in pain, scared, and confused. I was pulled out of school, forced to leave my home, and had to live in a psychiatric ward for months because no one took the time to listen to what I had to say about what was happening to me. The entire ordeal taught me to be an advocate for myself. In doing so, I attained the strength and courage to refuse any of the unjust and inaccurate labels others attempted to place on me.

Blind Hope

As a youth, I was a bit rebellious. After a disagreement I had with someone at work, I was very upset and needed to leave. My boss called Bishop to pick me up. During the car ride home, a stern lecture ensued, but I barely heard a word of it. Frustrated with my attitude, Bishop gave me the option to leave if I could not comply with his rules. Without pause, I surrendered my keys and went up to my friend's job at Dunkin Donuts. A few hours passed before the police cars showed up. Scared that the police were there to look for me, I walked back over to Burger King where I worked to speak with my manager about using his car. I had my driver's license and he was insured, so he didn't see a problem with loaning me his car.

I drove over to my uncle's house and chilled for a little while. Upon my arrival, I learned that my parents had already called there looking for me. When my parents called there again, they discovered that I was there and rushed right over. While my cousin was getting lectured for not telling my great-aunt that I was there, I snuck out with the car and left without being seen. I drove back to Burger King and returned the car to my manager. My parents realized that I was gone and came to Burger King. I rode home with them. Well, they weren't too pleased with my behavior. Once we got home, I threw some clothes in a bag and had my grandmother pick me up to take me back to her house. At the age of 17, I was officially out of their home.

My parents wanted me to go to the prom at our church instead of the one at my school. I didn't want to miss out on the experience and decided to go to my school's prom. Although my parents didn't see me off, my grandmother did. We took her Cadillac and had a great time. My date was my best friend, who was a college sophomore. He had asked me to go with him to prom two years prior, but my parents only consented to the dance, not after prom or any of the other festivities, so I had to turn him down. I was glad to have the opportunity to share such a special time with him. **I was happy to win another round in my life! It's important to also count the small victories in life, no matter how small.**

Kimberly Holmes

Highlight Reel: My teen years were a time in my life when I craved independence. After having two children of my own, I now realize that I was no different than any other teenager. But, at the time, my parents made me feel like my behavior was completely unacceptable. I now know that it was necessary to go through that process in order to find my own way. I'm a much better person today for it.

Exercise 5:1

Bird Set Free: Have you ever felt caged in by someone or something–like you just needed to break free for your own sanity? Whether the restriction was intentional or not, if it made you feel uncomfortable or repressed, it was not for your benefit. How did you find the courage to free yourself? Journal about your growth since then.

_____
_____
_____
_____
_____
_____
_____
_____
_____
_____
_____
_____
_____
_____
_____
_____
_____
_____
_____
_____

Exercise 5:2

Closing a Chapter: Have you ever had the opportunity to revisit a situation that you had to walk away from in the past? Was it a relationship, an opportunity, or a position? How did it feel to pursue the closure for that situation?

_____
_____
_____
_____
_____
_____
_____
_____
_____
_____
_____
_____
_____
_____
_____
_____
_____
_____
_____
_____
_____
_____
_____
_____
_____
_____
_____
_____
_____
_____

Pulling on My Mommy Gloves

A month after prom, I graduated from high school. The following year, I met my boyfriend and later became a mother at the age of 19 to a beautiful boy named Xavier. It wasn't until I became pregnant with my daughter the following year that I experienced pregnancy complications. I was sick during the entire pregnancy. Due to severe preeclampsia, I was hospitalized, and I asked to deliver her six weeks early. I distinctly remember lying on the operating table for several hours because they couldn't find a vein to give me fluids. As a result, they inserted a central line catheter and I was given an epidural. On November 14th, my baby girl was brought into this world. I remember feeling the pressure and seeing the back of her head, which was full of curly, black hair. I was informed by the OB-GYN of how dangerous the delivery procedure had been. He informed me that I would die if I had another child and that I should seriously consider having my tubes tied. I respectfully declined his offer, refusing to accept that I couldn't have another child. God has the final say. Then I passed out cold.

Although I had two children with my significant other, I knew that I still wanted to get married one day. I wanted to have the option to have children the correct way — with a husband — and did not want a doctor who barely knew me to make that decision for us. When the time came, we would have that conversation together.

While I was pregnant with my daughter, my children's father cheated on me. If that wasn't bad enough, I later found out that the other woman was expecting with his child. The babies would be ten months apart. While I was in labor, he refused to come up to the hospital to see me. After my daughter was born, she was nameless for two weeks because I was deathly ill, and her father did not come to meet her or visit me. His mother was supportive and would give him money for gas and he still did not come. He was living with his future child's mother at the time and did not want to be bothered with us any longer.

For two long weeks, I fought for my life, knowing that I had a young son and brand-new daughter to raise. Bishop, who was a minister at the time, would visit and pray over my daughter and me regularly. He would rub her with oil and advocate on her behalf when I couldn't. Despite the health complications I had during my pregnancy with my daughter, I believed everything would work out just fine. My faith along with the love and support of my family were all I had to hold on to at that time. What was supposed to be one of the happiest times of my life was overcast with the absence of my children's father, his neglect for our family, and my failing health. The doctors didn't expect me to live, but I refused to give up. I had a lot to live for. I was in and out of consciousness, but I do remember my children's father entering my hospital room and waking me up.

He asked, "What do you want to name her?"

I told him that I hadn't thought of any names yet.

So he asked, "What do you think of Shiara?"

I said, "Oh, that's cool," and fell back asleep, still heavily sedated.

Thanks to the Lord and my family's prayers and good thoughts, my health eventually improved enough for my mother to wheel me downstairs to see Shiara. Seeing her made the struggle and pain worth it and I never had a single regret. I began learning things about my daughter, such as her lactose intolerance. Having her in a separate room was an adjustment. While in the hospital, Xavier was right in the room with me. But I would go down and hold her, feed her a bottle and sing to her. All I wanted was to see her healthy and happy.

Just before Thanksgiving, I was all set to go home – until they found blood in Shiara's stool. They had to keep her for a week after I was released. I would call her father, asking him to take me to the hospital to visit Shiara, but to no avail. The father of my children, who had chosen their names, refused to comply.

A few days after Thanksgiving, I finally brought Shiara home. However, our joyful reunion was short-lived. At her follow-up appointment, we discovered she had a heart murmur and was developing severe asthma issues. Despite Shiara's issues with asthma, heart murmurs, and pneumonia, nothing was enough to compel my ex to visit his newborn child. A combination of single motherhood, concern for my daughter's health, lack of rest, and the stress that comes with being a new mother caused my level of self-care to decline drastically. I spent most of my time monitoring the health of my children and advocating for their peace of mind. During the times in between, my last thoughts did not include insulin or any of the other medications I needed to remain healthy and stable. I would get sick, but I focused on Xavier and Shiara. Little did I know, my condition was silently worsening.

Recurring bouts of pneumonia kept Shiara in and out of the hospital. My family members watched Xavier whenever I rushed Shiara back and forth to the hospital. She was an itty-bitty, frail thing and didn't begin walking until she was almost 18 months old. Her pediatrician and specialists said she would not be able to walk at all because her weight remained in the 12-15-pound range. If you've learned anything about me so far, you may have predicted that I respectfully refused to accept their prognosis for my baby. As it turned out, so did my little Shiara.

One day while in church service, Bishop was giving his sermon when his attention suddenly focused on Shiara.

He told the church, "They said this baby would never walk!"

The congregation collectively verbalized their empathy.

He then looked up at me and said, "Kim. Sit the baby down in the aisle."

Without hesitation, I did as I was told. I lifted Shiara from my lap and walked over to the aisle, then gently placed her on the floor. She sat up and gazed all around her.

"They said this baby would never walk!" Bishop repeated.

I watched along with the congregation as Shiara reached a tiny hand up to a pew arm and pulled herself up. Then she confidently took her very first steps. I joyfully witnessed my baby enter and dance victoriously around her very own ring. **Yet another prognosis blocked, and I didn't even have to fight in this bout!** I expect a miracle every day and that was the best one yet.

Shortly afterward, Shiara was back in the hospital with pneumonia. As I previously stated, her pediatrician formerly doubted her ability to walk due to her frail state. Given the doubtful nature of his prognosis, I decided to switch insurance plans and found another doctor for a second opinion at another hospital. I am an optimistic person who actively seeks out like-minded people. I wanted my family to be under the care of people who keenly weigh all the available options in their advisement. In a meeting with the chief pediatric cardiologist, he confirmed that Shiara's heart surgery should have been performed at a few days after she was born. She was three at the time. That was all the confirmation I needed. He personally performed her surgery. Since having the surgery, Shiara has not experienced any more heart-related complications. **Prognosis blocked! We had won that round together!**

Highlight Reel: From a complicated pregnancy to the betrayal of cheating from my significant other to dealing with health issues to neglecting my own health to ensure my daughter had what she needed ... I think it would be safe to say that was quite a difficult time in my life. It all wound down to protecting my child at all costs. When you learn that you're going to become a parent, you always hope that you will be able to give your children everything they need. I learned a lot about myself as a person and as a mother during that time.

Exercise 6:1

The Effect of Betrayal is Real: Have you ever felt betrayed or neglected by people in your life during a time of vulnerability or crisis? How did you get past it? Were you able to forgive them and move on? This is necessary in order to maintain happiness and fulfillment in your life. If you have yet to forgive who hurt you, start to think about the reasons why you haven't done so. Journal about the baby steps you can take to get to a place of forgiveness.

_____
_____
_____
_____
_____
_____
_____
_____
_____
_____
_____
_____
_____
_____
_____
_____
_____
_____
_____

Exercise 6:2

The Struggle is Real: Have you ever felt overwhelmed by the stress of your responsibilities? Dealing with financial problems, illness, or lack of time can be debilitating while trying to juggle other pressing commitments. If you find yourself in this situation, try to focus on how blessed you are to have this responsibility, whether it's children, a demanding job, or earning or maintaining someone's trust. Try your best to prioritize your tasks, ask for help/advice and, most of all, pray for guidance. Journal below about ways you can delegate or organize your tasks in a way that lessens your stress.

Round 7

It All Falls Down

I was grateful that both of my children were finally healthy and able to lead happy, normal lives. Things began to look up for me as well. I started a new job and was able to take care of my children and my household. But the elephant's presence was still lingering in the room: my own declining health.

A couple of years later, while working at Red Lobster, one of my co-workers approached me and asked why I was squinting at the computer screen.

I looked at him and said, "Boy, I can see just fine."

He said, "You should go to the doctor to make sure you're good."

I didn't think much of it afterward. I started getting sick again, which, of course, was due to complications of my diabetes. I applied for disability benefits and was eventually sent to a specialist who diagnosed me with diabetic retinopathy, a common complication of diabetes due to damaged blood vessels in the retina of the eye. Diabetic retinopathy is hard to detect initially because there are usually no symptoms during the early onset of disease. As the disease progresses, mild vision impairment eventually leads to blindness in people with diabetes types 1 and 2.

Blind Hope

Since I developed diabetes at such a young age and went for prolonged periods of time neglecting my self-care, I was at a much higher risk of developing diabetic retinopathy. As if potentially losing my sight weren't enough, I later found out while visiting my primary care physician that I was having kidney complications as well. Diabetes can injure the small blood vessels in the kidney as well. Once the blood vessels in the kidneys are injured, it hinders their ability to clean the blood, resulting in the retention of water and salt, protein in the urine. As such, waste fragments remain in the blood.

Over time, I struggled with seeing clearly. I even found myself going into the drug store to purchase reading glasses to help my vision. Regardless of the hindrance of my sight, I decided to follow my dreams and enroll in medical assisting school. It wasn't easy and there were times when I struggled to do the work and make it back and forth to class. But nothing motivated me more than achieving my goal and proving my naysayers wrong. With diligence, determination, and sheer grit, I pressed on and successfully finished the program. I had naysayers in my life who asked me why I had enrolled in school. They told me that I would struggle with my program and that it was a waste of my time and money. **Negative projections blocked!**

When driving, I began experiencing difficulty seeing in bright sunlight. I could see clearly but could not determine the color of the traffic light. Once I realized this, I followed the car ahead or asked my children what color the traffic light was. After discovering that I was no longer able to make the color distinction, I chose to only drive when it was cloudy or rainy outside to avoid putting myself and others in danger. One rainy and dreary day, I got off the highway and pulled to a stop at the light. I was able to clearly see that it was a red light. Once the light changed to green, I prepared to move forward, but suddenly felt the wheel jerk to the right, as if I had done it involuntarily. After a second of confusion, I looked up to see a motorcycle directly in front of me, which I had not noticed before *at all*. I collected my bearings and allowed my heart to return to its normal rhythm before proceeding through the light. It was at that moment that I realized that it was God Who had guided me to avoid hitting the motorcyclist. That was my confirmation that it was time for me to stop driving altogether.

During my freshman year in high school, I was allowed to work in the nurse's office during study hall period. It was during that time that I decided to become an advocate for others. I began researching the details of a neo-natal nurse career. I wanted to work in the Neonatal Intensive Care Unit (NICU). I enrolled in a nursing program at Notre Dame and made it a year into the program but had to withdraw due to my sight issues.

Later that year, I began having stomach complications. I couldn't keep anything down and was vomiting on a regular basis. Once I ate something that aggravated my stomach, the purging began and would not stop. It was alarming because no matter what I tried, I could not keep much of anything down. This went on for months until I was diagnosed with gastroparesis, a digestive condition characterized by stomach paralysis. We discovered that the food I ate would sit in my stomach for longer than the average timeframe because nerves and muscles in my digestive track were damaged as a result of my diabetes. It became an unfortunate trend that all of my complications were a direct result of my uncontrolled sugar levels in the past. My doctor put me on anti-nausea medication, which did not help. Taking full responsibility for my condition, I took a more active stance in analyzing my diet. I conducted some research and learned that staying away from foods that were high in fiber and fat was essential. Consuming those foods only extended my digestion process.

In addition to gradually losing my sight and dealing with the gastroparesis, in October of 2005, I began dialysis for treatment of my kidney deterioration. The dialysis was designed to cleanse my blood of the impurities that built up over time. They installed an arteriovenous fistula in my arm to provide a smoother process. Despite the near 95% success rate for this procedure, it did not work for me. So, they decided to install a catheter in my chest for the dialysis process. In the meantime, I was unable to keep food down. But life pressed on.

Blind Hope

In August 2006, my children started school – Xavier was in first grade, and Shiara was in kindergarten. I remember the two of them rushing home to show me what they had worked on in school and handing me important papers, but all I could see was a blur. I couldn't see clearly enough to make out the words. I had to ask the teachers to print their notes to me instead of writing in cursive so that Xavier could read them to me. I experienced guilt because I felt like my children had to grow up faster than they should have. One example was a night that I had just gotten home from being hospitalized and had the children with me. My blood sugar level was extremely low because I had been vomiting. I struggled to make it over to the kitchen to try to get something to eat. I was reaching for something on the top shelf of the refrigerator when I felt my vision darken and my body weaken. On my way down to the floor, I weakly called out, "Help me," before I blacked out.

Unbeknownst to me, I had officially tagged my son to enter the ring and fight on my behalf. I was no longer able to defend myself and needed someone else to fight my battle. Xavier had been standing ringside with his little boots laced, pounding his gloves together, and cheering me on the whole time. He stepped in, light on his feet, and eager to fight for me.

I had already trained my children by showing them how to dial 9-1-1 in case of a medical emergency. Xavier immediately made his way over to the phone and made the call. He made sure Shiara got dressed before the paramedics arrived. When I came to, the police and paramedics were there, ready to transport me back to the hospital. Six-year-old Xavier handed the keys to one of the police officers and said, "Make sure you lock my Mommy's door." I smiled as I listened to my baby Xavier. **It was our first official tag team and he killed his first round! I was beyond proud.**

Due to the bright sunlight, something as simple as walking my children to the bus stop in the morning became a laborious task as I could barely focus. I would either have to wait for the sun to go behind a cloud or ask the children to let me know when they reached the stop safely. Eventually, a neighbor offered to walk my children to the stop upon taking note of how frequently the paramedics came to my doorstep.

The more time that passed, the more I felt like a burden on my family and friends. I felt helpless as I lain in bed in agony, barely able to get up to take care of myself. In my mind, I brought it all on myself because I failed to take care of myself properly. I would order food and cook enough for the kids to have something to eat, but Xavier would have to set it out for himself and his sister. My great-aunt, who was in her 70s, would come over to help as much as she could, but she had her own household and job to manage.

Due to my deteriorating physical condition and my reluctance to contact my loved ones when I needed assistance, I was eventually deemed unfit to care for my own children. Consequently, they admitted me to a nursing facility and was placed on a double transplant list for kidneys and a new pancreas. **I took a bolo jab that time, which is a punch used to distract you from the real blow.** It never crossed my mind that the care I provided for my children was unfit. I was simply doing the best I could with what I had. I suffered miserably as a result of poor defense. **But the blow didn't knock me out. I stayed in the ring. But the fight wasn't over yet.**

That was one of the most difficult times of my life. Not only was my illness getting the best of me, but I was also torn away from my children and my home and stuck in a strange place against my will. I was physically and emotionally exhausted and felt helpless. My children were with their dad, and I later found out they were experiencing mental, verbal, and emotional abuse by him and his wife. They would tell my children I didn't want them or love them and that I had left them behind. My children's father would pass the nursing facility every day on his way to his mother's house and still would not bring the kids to visit me. He claimed that he didn't have enough gas to make the visit, so I began sending him gas money. Even gas money wasn't enough to convince him to do the right thing and let me see my children. I requested for my children to call me, but he claimed that he didn't have phone bill money. I sent over cell phones for my children to use to call me and still did not hear from them. There were two adults and six children in the household, and

I later found out they would often miss meals due to a lack of money in their household.

Highlight Reel: It felt like everything around me was crumbling. Not one area of my life was functioning properly. My body was attacking itself and it felt as though there was a war going on inside of me. Despite my pain, I attempted to maintain a stable home for my children because I did not want to become a burden to others in my life.

The biggest blow was having to leave my household and my children to live in the nursing facility. Not only was I away from my babies, but I also had to give up my independence and face the fact that I could not take care of things on my own. I was still young, yet I felt like an elderly invalid.

I then found out that my children were living in an undesirable environment. If I've ever felt like throwing in the towel in my life, it was during that time. But I refused to give up. I remained focused on getting my children what they needed and keeping a positive mindset. I knew that the more positive I was about my situation, the better my chances of recovery.

Exercise 7:1

Going Through It to Get to It: Have you ever felt like bad news was raining down on you relentlessly? Have you ever been slapped in the face with more bad news as soon as you've finished processing something troublesome or stressful? How did you handle the stress, grief, or fear? Did moving past it take forgiveness, faith, or counseling? List the lessons you learned as a result as well as the ways you're greater for enduring it.

_____
_____
_____
_____
_____
_____
_____
_____
_____
_____
_____
_____
_____
_____
_____
_____
_____
_____
_____
_____

Exercise 7:2

Silver Lining: Have you ever struggled to find something positive in a situation that was extremely dark and hopeless? Did you rely on the support and encouragement of others to reach this point or were you forced to find the silver lining on your own? Pat yourself on the back for staying positive and making your way through it. Journal about your experience below.

The Fade to Black

Each day that passed in the nursing facility, I would lie in my bed, feeling sick and in pain. One day, I woke up to total darkness. I blinked a few times and rubbed my eyes slowly, thinking it might be the middle of the night. But when I turned my face toward the hall, I didn't see the light leaking in under the door. I couldn't make out any silhouettes in the room either. After a few moments of bewilderment, I realized that I was completely blind. I was terrified. I remember thinking, "Oh, well, I can't see anything now."

My vision had already been clouded for quite a while, so it was an eventual transition that I knew was coming. But I don't think anything can fully prepare you for blindness. I took that time to silently reflect on the events of my life. I forgave others who had wronged and hurt me, and I forgave myself for my past transgressions. It was at that time that I made peace with everything in my life and was able to move forward with a clean slate and heart. **That was a very hard blow to the face.** But I found the ability to move forward in a positive way while accepting what I could not change. Being blind became an important and influential factor in my life.

I would often get sick during my dialysis treatments. So, my routine would look like this: from the nursing facility to dialysis, to the hospital, and back to the nursing facility. At one point, my weight decreased to as little as 99 pounds. I didn't want to eat anything other than salads. My mother came in one day after speaking to a minister who anointed a cloth with oil. The minister informed my mother that I would get better and to keep the faith. She also relayed the message from the minister for me to pray while holding the cloth and to take it everywhere I went. I happily complied. Doing so brought me comfort and strength during such a trying time.

A month later, I received a call from the hospital that informed me that organs had been found for me. I was elated and overjoyed. Once I got to the hospital, however, we discovered that the organs weren't in good condition, so they sent me back to the nursing facility.

I was devastated, but not deflated. I continued to pray with my anointed cloth, keeping the faith that what the Lord had for me was only for me. A few months later, the hospital called again to announce that more organs had been found for me. This time, I was unable to accept the organs due to being hospitalized for complications from my gastroparesis. For the second time, I had to pass on the organs. This time, they went to the next person in line. Although I was disappointed that I missed the opportunity, I was relieved that I remained at the top of the list. Meanwhile, I was still suffering from diabetes-related issues. The next time they called, I smiled to myself and remained confident that it would work out. It was nighttime and I was more than ready to receive the good news. I said to myself, "Third time's a charm." I called my family and told them to be ready to come to the hospital. I had a good feeling about all of it.

The staff at the nursing facility ordered transportation for me and I made my way over to the hospital. I underwent dialysis at 5 a.m. to ensure that my blood was clean and that my body was ready to receive the healthy organs. The doctor gave his approval that I was all set to undergo the procedure. My entire family was there, lending their support before I went into surgery. After my surgery, they all came into my room, two by two, to pray with me and give their well wishes.

I asked the doctor to give me a little bit of background on my donor, as I would be walking around with the donor's organs in my body. I came to find out that my donor was the victim of a car accident and the family decided to donate the organs. The donor was 29 years old, just like me. I also had the transplant on the 29th of January. The trinity of numbers was a good sign.

It was a great moment in my life. **Although I won that round**, I felt like I had lost.

I felt an overwhelming sadness because my children were missing from my supportive circle of family.

Highlight Reel: Losing my sight and missing out on receiving donated organs twice was very difficult for me to get through. **I was taking some massive blows in the ring.** As the storm continued, I remained committed to keeping the faith and holding onto a positive frame of mind. I had loved ones encouraging me and, despite my blindness, I never lost sight of my children, who were my main sources of motivation to keep fighting. Regardless of what I endured, I knew that there would be no nursing facility in my future. My bigger picture was all about my children and creating a happy, healthy home for them.

Exercise 8:1

Moving Mountains: Think of the biggest obstacle you have had to face in your life. Are you proud of how you handled the challenge? Is there anything you would have done differently? How did it prepare you for future challenges?

_____
_____
_____
_____
_____
_____
_____
_____
_____
_____
_____
_____
_____
_____
_____
_____
_____
_____
_____
_____
_____
_____

Exercise 8:2

Doubt: During a dark time in your life, have you ever found yourself questioning God or your own abilities to make it through? How did you pull through the process in order to find the light? Now that you've made it through, what about those experiences are you most thankful for?

The Rebirth

Meanwhile, children services discovered that my children were living in an abusive and dangerous environment with their father, his wife, and her children. Shiara was carrying some trash outside and cut her ankle on the glass from one of her father's beer bottles. While visiting with their paternal grandmother, she noticed her injury. When she asked Shiara why she was walking funny, she broke down and told her everything. Both of my children were threatened not to tell anyone outside of the household anything about the abuse they were experiencing under their father's care.

Post-surgery life was complicated. I was only supposed to have a seven-to-ten-day recovery period. However, I couldn't get up and walk around, despite the doctor and nurses' repeated requests. I would sleep all the time and I was still experiencing severe stomach pains. I was concerned about my body rejecting the donated kidney, but the medical staff assured me that I was doing fine and healing nicely. In their minds, there was no reason for me to be bedridden with pain. Once again, I had to advocate for myself and insist that something was wrong. I knew my body, and something was still off. I shouldn't have been feeling that way if the procedure was successful. After being examined, they discovered that I had an abscess on my newly implanted kidney. I had to go back into the operating room for emergency surgery to remove the abscess.

What should have been a week's stay in the hospital turned into a month. I finally began to experience some relief, but it was overshadowed by the onset of yet another round in the ring for me. The first issue was while I attempted to get out of the bed and tried walking around. Once I was firmly on my feet, I discovered that I had forgotten how! I spent so much time in the hospital, I had to learn how to walk all over again. I was still having stomach issues, so my weight was at a mere 99 pounds and my muscles were severely weak, which leads me to the second issue. I had a feeding tube installed - for the second time in my life - to try to increase my weight and strength during my recovery. My third issue was securing living arrangements for myself. I did not want to live at the nursing facility. Bishop believed it was in my best interest to return to the nursing facility for observation, so I reached out to my great-aunt. She was unable to help me at the time because she had plans to be out of town soon. Consequently, I found myself back in the nursing facility for the time being.

I must admit, I was on the ropes, y'all. After overcoming the multiple-round fight to get well enough to receive my organs, I then had to endure a lengthy post-transplant recovery period. Once I finally saw the light at the end of the tunnel in leaving the nursing facility, I felt as if I was on track to getting back to a normal life. However, God saw fit to send me back to the nursing facility, which proved to be a bit much for me to swallow.

I stayed at the nursing facility for six additional months until my great-aunt returned from her trip and got settled. I moved in with her shortly afterward.

My seventy-something-year-old great-aunt juggled hosting me in her home, figuring out my feeding tube machine, and rushing me back and forth to the hospital. I was still vomiting and lost an additional ten pounds, and I remember Bishop having to carry me to the car and into the hospital to help my great-aunt. Sitting up was painful because of my severe fat and muscle loss and I had to go to a rehab center. Not much time had passed since my surgery; in fact,

Blind Hope

I still had the staples in my stomach. My skin had actually grown over them because no one had bothered to remove them. I guess all my other complications had taken precedence over removing the staples. In the meantime, I began receiving physical and occupational therapy and was eventually taken off the feeding tube. My great-aunt was elated to hear the news about my feeding tube being removed as she was excited to finally have the opportunity to fatten me up. She busied herself cooking all types of food and tried to get me to eat all the time, even though I wasn't hungry. I tried to educate her about my condition by giving her brochures and other information, but she still insisted that I eat. She even called my parents, upset that she couldn't get me to eat anything.

The onset of blindness left my eyes discolored. I started going to the Cleveland Sight Center to learn more occupational skills in preparation for living independently with my children. I even learned Braille. I met people that were blind and some were also deaf, due to illness and brain trauma. It was inspiring to bond with people who understood the stigmas we faced each day. They understood the alienation and the limitations placed on us due to our inability to see. I even rekindled a friendship with someone who knew me from our summer camp days. She was six years older than I am, but she recognized my laugh from twenty years ago. She remembered every detail of who I was, and it was great to connect with her again.

In 2009, a group of us from the Cleveland Sight Center traveled to Detroit for the National Federation of the Blind's National Convention. Unfortunately, I continued suffering from gastroparesis and all of the digestive issues that came with it. I got sick in my hotel room and had to be taken to the hospital in Detroit. It ended up being a waste of time and resources because they couldn't treat me due to a lack of knowledge concerning my condition. So, I endured a grueling two-and-a-half-hour ride home in an ambulance. Thankfully, my friends from the Cleveland Sight Center met my mother with my luggage. I love those ladies. We talk regularly to this day.

In early 2010, I was introduced to the idea of inserting a stomach pacer to contract my stomach muscles to help move the food along the digestive tract faster. The procedure would also decrease my nausea and vomiting. I conducted my research and eventually consented to have it implanted. In March of that year, I had the procedure done. Although optimistic that the procedure would work, I couldn't help but entertain some skepticism. It wasn't that I didn't trust my doctors and their skills; it was just that I had been through a lot already and was worried about what my quality of life would be if the procedure didn't work as planned. My persistent digestive issues kept me in and out of the hospital every two weeks and I was beyond tired of dealing with it. It was at that time that I made it my mission to actively change my diet in order to control my stomach flare-ups. It wasn't until 2016 that doctors figured out that gastroparesis, not food, was what triggered my stomach flare-ups.

Upon finally getting a diagnosis and placing a name on my mysterious condition, I did some research to better understand it. On May 24, 2018, I became the first one in Cleveland Clinic's patient history to have a stomach pacer removed. Although the pacer kept my weight steady at 135 pounds, the doctors determined that it was not serving its desired purpose and supported my decision to have it removed. Since the removal, I have actually gained weight. My appetite has increased and I feel much better now. This all came about because I made it a mission to advocate for myself.

During that time, I was friends with a guy who was very emotionally and physically supportive. He was there whenever I needed him and was always checking up on me to make sure I had what I needed. But there was a significant catch: he was ashamed to be seen with me. He cared about me and would do anything for me, except let the world know that we were friends. At the time, I was still learning about the stigmas associated with my condition. I knew how it affected me each day, but discovering the impact my condition had on others was something new for me.

Blind Hope

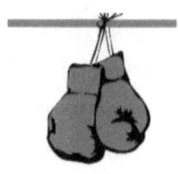 **Highlight Reel:** This was another period of my life where I had to fight again. I had to learn how to cope with my blindness, learn how to build new relationships, and learn how to read again, on top of fighting to maintain control of my health. It was a transitional period, but I knew that I still had a long way to go. Regardless, it felt good to finally be on my way.

Exercise 9:1

Back to the Start: Have you ever had to reprogram yourself and go back to the basics in life? Was this a result of needing a clean slate or was it just a need to be reborn? How did you remain positive through this process?

Exercise 9:2

New Friends: Have you found new friendships later in your life that have been just as purposeful as some of your older friendships? What common bond did you find that helped build your relationship? What purpose do you think they serve in your life's journey?

The Main Event...Getting My Kids Back

During my recovery period, my children went back and forth between living with my parents and their father. Altogether, it took me a total of five years to regain my independent status after going into the nursing facility.

I took braille classes at the Cleveland Sight Center, which enabled me to read and learned to utilize bump docks to gauge temperatures while cooking. I also learned to vacuum, wash clothes, and use a microwave without the use of my sight. I spent time with the kids during the holidays and during the summer while living with my great-aunt. My great-aunt and the Sight Center social worker took me around to look at houses. I got approved for a two-bedroom house right before the kids started school in August of 2011. My ex never filed for custody of the kids, so we didn't have to go through a long court battle for me to regain custody of them. I simply called and told him that I wanted to regain custody of the children. A couple of days later, I had my children back. He provided me with the documents I needed to get them enrolled in school.

Xavier and Shiara returned to me with minimal belongings. Most of the things I sent for them had been pawned for money. They came back with tattered clothes and shoes, despite all the quality items I'd sent over for them. I knew the kids didn't have the structure and guidance they needed while I was gone, so I was ready to enroll them in counseling and get them the support they needed to make the transition between households as smoothly as possible. Unfortunately, neither of them was receptive to therapy. Adjusting to living under the same roof together again was very difficult. Xavier was very angry and was acting out. He would have fits where he was inconsolable and would destroy my property.

By 2015, I chose to send Xavier back to live with his father so that he could graduate with his friends. He still had some issues, but he graduated. After graduation, he came back to live with me. Xavier experienced homelessness after his father kicked him out, which forced him to live between his friends' homes. Thankfully, he was in a healthier emotional state and even apologized for his past behavior. I was proud to see him take accountability for his actions and display empathy for my situation.

Although I was grateful to be on my own again with my children back at home with me, I was still dealing with some pertinent issues. Soon after I moved out of her home, my great-aunt was diagnosed with colon cancer. I called for a transportation service to take me to visit her. The driver who picked me up that day was very nice. He mentioned how independent I seemed to be, despite my condition. I felt accomplished because I had my own place, had gotten my kids back, and I was doing my best to provide a safe and happy home for them. It wasn't easy because they were older with their own issues to deal with. We were all trying to figure out how to co-exist happily and healthily together as a functional family.

The driver also complimented me on my appearance and, although I thanked him for his kind words, my mind was somewhere entirely different. I was worried about my great-aunt, my health, and my children. While my kids were in school, I traveled back and forth to my great-aunt's house, making sure she had what she needed. Unfortunately, in August of 2012 my great-aunt passed away.

In 2013 I was still involved with the guy who was ashamed of being seen with me in public. In hindsight, I believe that I wanted to prove to him that I was worthy of being seen. But I had to come to understand that my worth is not something I should ever have to prove to anyone. I bring love, support, and encouragement, among many other things, to my relationships. If that wasn't good enough for him, then that should have been my immediate cue to leave him alone.

One day, a few years later, I stepped onto the bus and heard a familiar voice greet me. I wasn't sure who it was at first, but as he engaged me in conversation, I realized it was the same driver who had complimented me three years prior. This time, he was determined to pursue a friendship with me. He asked me out on a date and, with the loose ends of my life tied up, I was finally at a point where I could focus on developing a new relationship. I was also looking forward to moving on from past unhealthy relationships. Derek is kind, thoughtful, and respectful and his heart is pure. He has been loving, supportive, reliable and, most of all, he is proud to walk beside me–anywhere we go. We are still together and are happily pursuing our common goals and enjoying all that life has to offer. He holds my hand through all the ups and downs and is right by my side, as an integral part of all the things I am. I've never been happier and I'm very optimistic about our future.

In 2018, I created my organization, Blind Hope LLC to provide support for those who face challenges in their lives. Through Blind Hope, my goal is to establish and maintain support groups that provide encouragement for those who are facing issues such as disabilities, lack of a supportive network, and other basic life issues. This will be a judgment-free space for those who would like to share their stories and receive sound advice from people who have been where they are. I was motivated to start Blind Hope because I have felt alone while suffering from afflictions. I lacked the ability to communicate with my family about what I was going through because they didn't understand what I was experiencing. My goal is to help people to find the resources they need as well as confront and communicate their obstacles without feeling ashamed, frustrated, or discouraged.

I have always been a firm believer that if it does not yet exist, then it should be your mission to help create it. I just want to do my part.

Time to Train

You should never be comfortable where you are. You should always strive to better yourself. Try to remember that God always has something better in store for you. When you dream, be sure to set goals and action items along with them to make them happen. Failing to pair action items with your goals will keep you stagnant, or worse, force you to regress back to previous unhealthy mindsets. And you don't want or need that!

Wisdom comes at all ages. Any time someone can teach you something, listen, watch, and learn. If nothing else, it's a life experience that you can benefit from and something you can add to your toolbox for future use. I have assembled some of the tools in my life that have never led me wrong. Hopefully, you can find value in my advice and pass it on to someone else.

Best Practices for Developing and Maintaining a Positive Mindset

① Before you react, always try to look for the good in each bad situation
② Eliminate the word "can't" from your vocabulary – just don't use it
③ Invest your time and efforts in self-empowerment
④ Remove naysayers from your life that try to derail you from focusing on your goals
⑤ Be diligent about keeping positive people around you for encouragement
⑥ Redirect any negativity you come across immediately
⑦ Be your own best cheerleader
⑧ Always be thankful* for your opportunities and what you have achieved thus far
⑨ Don't allow others' agendas or insecurities to interfere with your faith in yourself

*Remember that there is someone else who would love to have the opportunities that you have

Best Practices for Success

1. Adopt a solution-oriented mindset to work through your obstacles
2. Set goals that will empower you to improve yearly
3. When it comes to casting blame, always look within yourself first
4. Become self-confident and self-reliant through education and self-study
5. Focus on paving the way and being a light for others
6. Utilize your resources and the knowledge of your family and friends
7. Research everything you plan to do thoroughly before taking action
8. Share your knowledge and experience with others
9. Trust your intuition and judgment of character
10. When it comes to others, watch, don't listen. It's easier to talk the talk than it is to walk the walk. Ironically, I learned the importance of "watching" people more after I lost my sight

The Recap

Well, there you have it. This may not have been the fight of the century, but it has been a life-altering fight that has motivated me, my children, and some of my spectators on the sidelines. Although I am still battling the complications of my diabetes every day, I now have the confidence to step outside of the ring as a victor. I am fully aware of my worth, what I deserve, and what I expect from myself and others. I have made it my mission to empower and uplift others through positive affirmations, speaking engagements, and writing this book. No matter what happens from this point on, I know that I have fought a long, hard, and emotional fight and I have gone the distance. I hold my championship belt up high, knowing that my title can never be taken away from me.

I have gone pound for pound and round for round facing some very fierce opponents. And you know what? If you are reading my story, it means you want to know more about my personal life struggles. It means that you may be dealing with a struggle of your own and may need some encouragement to see it through. My advice to you is to know that no matter what it is you are facing – whether it is a long-term or short-term obstacle, it **does not have you**. The weight you carry on your shoulders doesn't matter. You will emerge as a victor, as long as your mind and heart are secure. You have no control over what happens to you in this life, but you have full control of your reactions to the obstacles that occur in your life.

I am a living testament that keeping a positive frame of mind not only increases your odds for success, but also elevates your physical health and your state of mind. Remember to wake up each morning with gratitude for the opportunity to make things right in your life. There are plenty who cannot claim the same.

Lastly, don't forget that your struggles aren't in vain. You may not like what you encounter during the storm, but you can always learn something from what comes from it. Don't give up. There is nothing you can't bear and if you are aware of this, you will be undefeated and arise as a stronger, wiser, and more determined fighter. It's the fight you were destined to have because, sometimes, you just have to go through to get to.

Peace and Blessings,
Champion Fighter,
Kimberly "The In*sight*ful" Holmes

About the Author

Kimberly Holmes is a motivational speaker and diabetes awareness advocate. She has spoken at the Cleveland Sight Center, Ursuline College, and John Carroll on her diabetes journey. She actively volunteers with LifeBanc, which provided her with the organs that saved her life. She founded the Blind Hope supportive program in late 2018 for those who face challenges with disabilities and other life-altering issues.

She lives in Cleveland, Ohio with her boyfriend and two children. This is her first book.

To book Kimberly for a speaking engagement on overcoming adversity, self-empowerment, and self-advocacy, living with diabetes, parenting while disabled, or adjusting to the outside world after diagnosis, please contact us at blindhopellc@gmail.com.

www.ingramcontent.com/pod-product-compliance
Lightning Source LLC
Chambersburg PA
CBHW030913170426
43193CB00009BA/838